# Wild ANIMAL Families

FUSION

# GRASSLAND
## ANIMAL GROUPS

by
**Rebecca Phillips-Bartlett**

**BEARPORT**
PUBLISHING

Minneapolis, Minnesota

**Credits**

All images are courtesy of Shutterstock.com, unless otherwise specified. With thanks to Getty Images, Thinkstock Photo, and iStockphoto. Recurring images – Cattallina, SunshineVector, ClassicVector, Amanita Silvicora, Sensvector, Miceking, A7880S. Cover – Claudia Paulussen, pandapaw, MrLis, Richard Juilliart. 2–3 – Volodymyr Burdiak, Maquiladora. 4–5 – Arturo de Frias, Maciej Czekajewski. 6–7 – JaySi, kungfoofoto, Lillac, Maciej Czekajewski, Winston Springwater, Traveller70, Greens and Blues, kavram. 8–9 – Victor Tyakht, Lara_day, Mikhail Gnatkovskiy. 10–11 – Ondrej Prosicky, Sainam51, Ihor Biliavskyi, Rimma R, Toni Genes, Sourabh Bharti, Shchipkova Elena. 12–13 – KenCanning, David Steele, Michael Potter11, Paul Hampton, Maquiladora, Tabby Mittins. 14–15 – Francois van Heerden, lumen-digital, Gary C. Tognoni, GraphicsRF.com, MPH Photos, Alfmaler, GranTotufo. 16–17 – fullempty, Oleg Znamenskiy, Wirestock Creators, MVshop, DanSzabo. 18–19 — Christoph Hilger, Craig Fraser, Volodymyr Burdiak, Alfmaler, Reto Buehler. 20–21 – :KenCanning, Stu Porter, Kirill Dorofeev, Ricardo Reitmeyer, GoodStudio. 22–23 – Igor Janicek, WOLF AVNI, ichywong, Sandiz, nipa74.

**Bearport Publishing Company Product Development Team**

President: Jen Jenson; Director of Product Development: Spencer Brinker; Managing Editor: Allison Juda; Associate Editor: Naomi Reich; Associate Editor: Tiana Tran; Senior Designer: Colin O'Dea; Associate Designer: Elena Klinkner; Associate Designer: Kayla Eggert; Product Development Assistant: Owen Hamlin

*Library of Congress Cataloging-in-Publication Data*

Names: Phillips-Bartlett, Rebecca, 1999- author.
Title: Grassland animal groups / Rebecca Phillips-Bartlett.
Description: Minneapolis, Minnesota : Bearport Publishing Company, [2024] | Series: Wild animal families | Includes index.
Identifiers: LCCN 2023028978 (print) | LCCN 2023028979 (ebook) | ISBN 9798889163213 (library binding) | ISBN 9798889163268 (paperback) | ISBN 9798889163305 (ebook)
Subjects: LCSH: Grassland animals--Juvenile literature.
Classification: LCC QL115.3 .P53 2024 (print) | LCC QL115.3 (ebook) | DDC 591.74--dc23/eng/20230713
LC record available at https://lccn.loc.gov/2023028978
LC ebook record available at https://lccn.loc.gov/2023028979

For more information, write to Bearport Publishing, 5357 Penn Avenue South, Minneapolis, MN 55419.

# CONTENTS

# WILD ANIMAL FAMILIES

Earth is full of amazing animals. Many of them live in groups. This can help animals stay safe. It makes it easier for them to find food and a place to stay.

Let's visit different animal families in the grasslands. This **habitat** has everything the plants and animals there need to live.

Many different wild families make their homes in grasslands.

# IN THE GRASSLANDS

Grasslands are flat, open spaces with low-growing grasses and plants. They do not get much rain.

Every **continent** except Antarctica has grasslands. They go by different names in different places. Grasslands are also called meadows, savannas, steppes (STEPZ), and prairies.

Grasslands have many grasses and flowers. There are very few trees.

7

# SAIGA ANTELOPES

The grasslands of Europe and Asia are home to saiga antelopes. These deerlike animals live in groups of about 30 to 40. But when they **migrate** a few times each year, the group size changes.

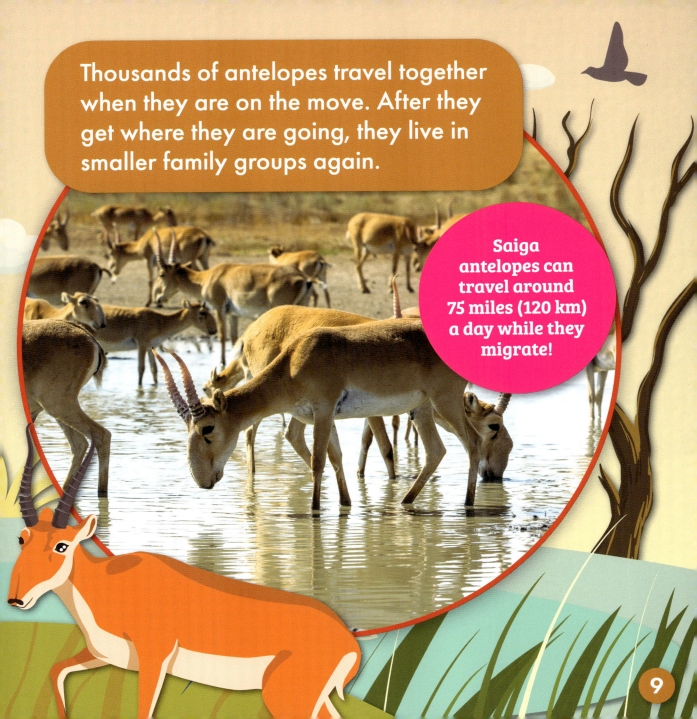

Thousands of antelopes travel together when they are on the move. After they get where they are going, they live in smaller family groups again.

Saiga antelopes can travel around 75 miles (120 km) a day while they migrate!

# STEPPE EAGLES

Steppe eagles also migrate in groups. When it is cold, they leave the steppes in Europe and Asia to travel to warmer places, such as African savannas.

During winter, steppe eagles often live near one another. They are also one of the only kinds of eagles that make their nests on the ground.

As they fly, steppe eagles spend very little time flapping their wings.

Baby steppe eagles in a nest

11

# AFRICAN ELEPHANTS

Elephants use their trunks to help calves.

African elephants are the world's largest land animals. They live in **female**-led groups known as herds or parades. Elephants in the parade work together to **support** everyone in the group.

During dry times of the year, elephants dig holes into **riverbeds**. In this way, they make watering holes. Other animals also use these watering holes.

# ZEBRAS

Zebras are some of the many kinds of animals that come together around watering holes. They live in family groups with about 5 to 20 animals. These families join together in herds known as dazzles.

Zebras work together to stay in a group. They will slow down to match the speed of the slowest member of the herd.

Zebras brush one another's fur using their teeth!

15

# OSTRICHES

Ostrich groups, called flocks, also look out for one another on the savanna. They use their amazing eyesight to watch for **predators**. Then, they let others know if they spot danger.

An ostrich's eye is bigger than its brain.

Ostriches live in flocks of around 12 birds. When it is time to lay eggs, all the mothers in the flock use the same nest. There can be more than 50 eggs in the nest!

Ostrich eggs

# GIRAFFES

Giraffes are so tall that a group of them is called a tower! Their height is very helpful in the grasslands. It gives them an excellent view of any nearby predators.

The giraffes in a tower take turns resting. There is always someone on the lookout.

Giraffes sometimes fight using their long necks.

# LIONS

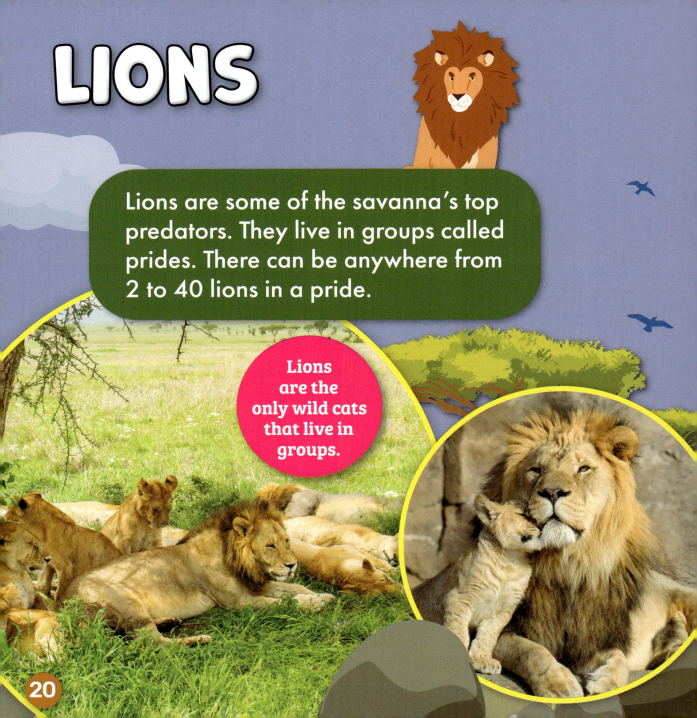

Lions are some of the savanna's top predators. They live in groups called prides. There can be anywhere from 2 to 40 lions in a pride.

Lions are the only wild cats that live in groups.

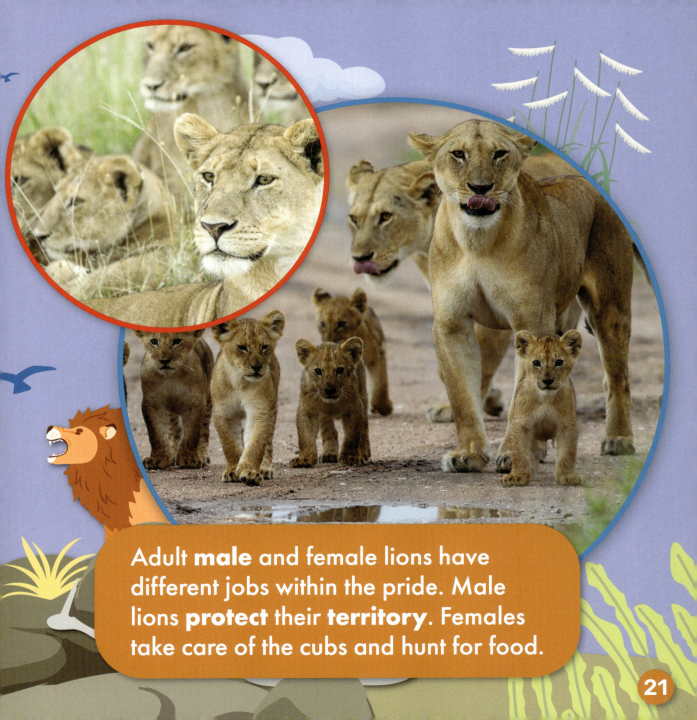

Adult **male** and female lions have different jobs within the pride. Male lions **protect** their **territory**. Females take care of the cubs and hunt for food.

# FAMILY FOCUS

Grasslands are home to many amazing animal family groups. These groups are all different in many ways. However, they do have some things in common.

Living in groups helps grassland animals face the challenges of their habitat. They come together to hunt food, fight off predators, and help one another as they migrate.

Which animal family group would you like to join?

# GLOSSARY

**continent** one of the world's seven large land masses

**female** an animal that can give birth or lay eggs

**habitat** a place in nature where a plant or animal normally lives

**male** an animal that cannot give birth or lay eggs

**migrate** to move from one place to another at a certain time of the year

**predators** animals that hunt and eat other animals

**protect** to keep safe

**riverbeds** the ground at the bottom of rivers, often ones that are dry

**support** to help and encourage

**territory** an area of land that belongs to and is defended by an animal or animal group

# INDEX